SUCCESS

Written By Rev. David Ibiayo

Illustrated By Russell Scott

Grosvenor House
Publishing Limited

I0079418

All rights reserved
Copyright © Rev. David Ibiayo, 2025

The right of Rev. David Ibiayo to be identified as the author of this
work has been asserted in accordance with Section 78
of the Copyright, Designs and Patents Act 1988

The book cover is copyright to Rev. David Ibiayo

This book is published by
Grosvenor House Publishing Ltd
Link House
140 The Broadway, Tolworth, Surrey, KT6 7HT.
www.grosvenorhousepublishing.co.uk

This book is sold subject to the conditions that it shall not, by way of
trade or otherwise, be lent, resold, hired out or otherwise circulated
without the author's or publisher's prior consent in any form of
binding or cover other than that in which it is published and
without a similar condition including this condition being
imposed on the subsequent purchaser.

This book is a work of fiction. Any resemblance to
people or events, past or present, is purely coincidental.

A CIP record for this book
is available from the British Library

Paperback ISBN 978-1-83615-030-5
Hardback ISBN 978-1-83615-031-2

davidibiayo@gmail.com

My wife (Oluwatomilola) and our daughters;
Lovely, Harmony, Prudence and Decency.

"............But as for me and my household,
we will serve the LORD."

Joshua 24:15

The following was said about Jesus Christ
when he was twelve years old.
"And Jesus grew in wisdom and stature,
and in favour with God and people."

Luke 2:52

I pray you grow in wisdom
as you read this book.

Rev. David Ibiayo

My name is ....
and I hope my journey through life is a success.

"A mindset of impossible
can never achieve what looks impossible."
Rev. David Ibiayo

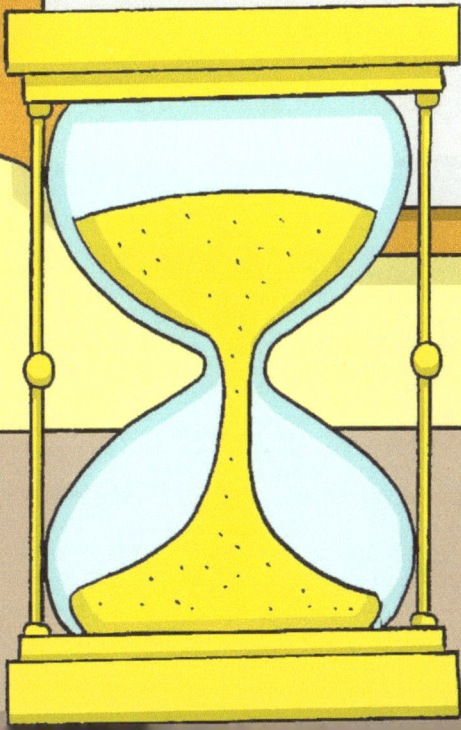

As Success set out on the road to seek a better future, he was met by Failure, who tried to discourage him. Failure said, "Some time ago, I set out on the road to seek a better future, but because of the challenges along the way, I quit. The journey demands perseverance and commitment which I did not have, and I was also advised by Discouragement that the journey wasn't worth it, because people hardly ever make it to their destination."

Success said to Failure,
"I can do everything through him who gives me strength." On hearing this, Failure walked away, and Success continued on his journey to seek a better future.

But before long, Success realised that he had not gone very far, because whenever he decided to plan the next steps of his journey, Laziness came along to keep him company, so he ended up doing nothing.

And by the time he managed to shake off Laziness and return to planning his journey, Distraction came along to keep him company; it was difficult to shake off Distraction, because Distraction got him involved in all the things he liked. Success preferred enjoying himself instead of planning his journey to seek a better future.

Foolishness also joined them in their enjoyment; he asked Success, "Why waste your time on a challenging journey when you can enjoy yourself?"

While Success was enjoying himself with Distraction and Foolishness, Discipline came along; seeing her made Success uncomfortable. Success could see in Discipline's eyes that she disapproved of what he was doing.

He asked Discipline, "Why don't you join us and have a good time?" Discipline declined and told him, "Ahead of this journey to a better future lies a time for fun, but for now you have to remain disciplined."

Distraction told Success not to listen to Discipline and that she was just a killjoy. At this point, Success asked Discipline to repeat what she had said. Discipline complied: "Ahead of this journey to a better future lies a time for fun, but for now you have to remain disciplined."

For a moment, it seemed as if
Distraction had managed to get
Success' attention, but when
Success heard the voice of Focus,
he asked Focus for his opinion.

Focus said to Success, "You remember that when you started your journey to seek a better future, you were focused, but now that you have become friends with Laziness and Distraction, where has that got you? You have not achieved your dream and, worse, you have lost your focus."

When Success heard Focus' words, he knew he had almost thrown away his dream of a better future; he came back to his senses and decided to dump Laziness and Distraction as friends and vowed never to keep company with Foolishness.

But Success was finding it hard to let go of Laziness and Distraction because they were very friendly with him and very nice to him. The temptation for him to keep Laziness and Distraction as his friends was really strong.

As Success sat down to think about how he was going to break away from Laziness and Distraction, Wisdom came along and had a word with him. She told Success that bad company corrupts good character and that you reap what you sow.

Wisdom asked him, "What kind of friends do you think would help you achieve your dream?" The question was a light bulb moment for Success, and he thanked Wisdom for her wise words and her question. Success then asked Discipline, Focus and Wisdom to be his friends.

Discipline, Focus and Wisdom told Success that it was not too late to continue his journey to seek a better future and that he could still achieve his dream, but that he needed to stay disciplined and focused.

As a result of this advice, Success
started to make his plans to seek
a better future and before long,
he was back on track.

At first, his journey to seek a better future seemed to be getting nowhere, but because of his discipline and focus, he started to cover ground, until he eventually reached his destination.

When he got to his destination, he remembered what Discipline had said to him: "Ahead of this journey to a better future lies a time for fun, but for now you have to remain disciplined."

There was a big smile on Success' face;
everybody was congratulating him on reaching his destination.

Someone in the crowd then shouted,
"Speech! Speech!" Success said, "I would like to thank God for making
me bear my cross and sending me three good friends, Discipline,
Focus and Wisdom, who spoke to me when I was going astray."

THIS IS WHAT INSPIRES US

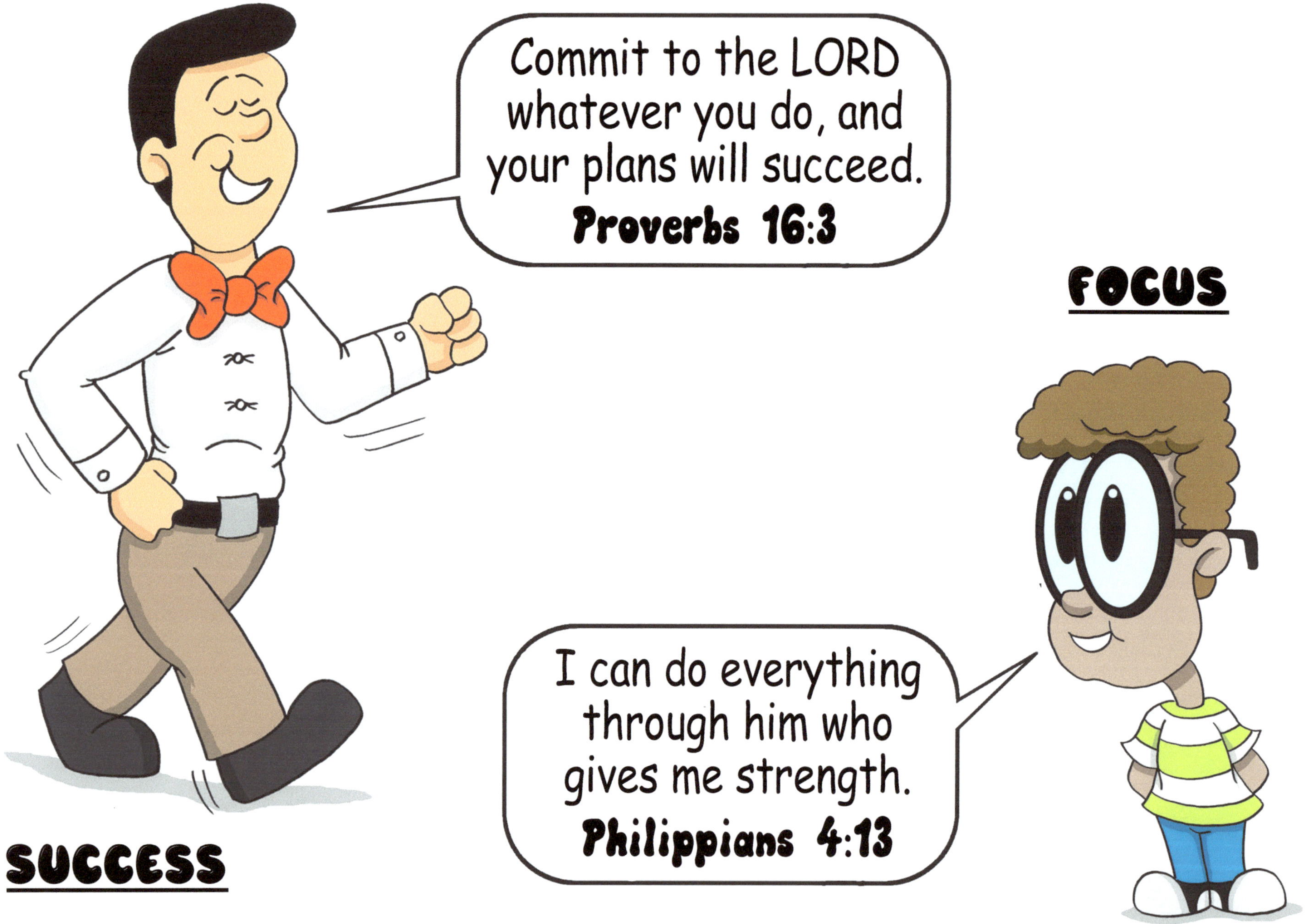

He who walks with the wise grows wise, but a companion of fools suffers harm. **Proverbs 13:20**

ARE THESE THE KIND OF FRIENDS YOU WANT TO BE AROUND YOU?
SUCCESS, FOCUS, WISDOM AND DISCIPLINE.

SUCCESS IS WITHIN YOUR REACH!

Look for the dotted line within the poem and write your name.

FAILURE OR SUCCESS?

What is the best way
to prepare for the future?
One of the ways
to prepare for the future
is to constantly
review your ROUTINE
(HOW ARE YOU SPENDING YOUR TIME DAILY?).

Tomorrow starts today!
If you don't put in the effort
and discipline yourself daily,
what do you think you will achieve
in the FUTURE; "TOMORROW?"

The book of Proverbs 6:9–11 has a warning for us;
"How long will you lie there, you sluggard?
When will you get up from your sleep?
A little sleep, a little slumber,
a little folding of the hands to rest –
and poverty will come on you like a bandit
and scarcity like an armed man."

Don't be sucked in by
relaxation, comfort and sleep;
as much as you need them,
you need to sacrifice them now and again:
The book of proverbs 16:26
urges you, ... to press on;
"The labourer's appetite works for him;
his hunger drives him on."

Do the right things daily
and you will have no regrets in the FUTURE:
The book of Proverbs 10:4
shows us the outcome
of being lazy or diligent;
"Lazy hands make a man poor,
but diligent hands bring wealth."

To achieve a goal demands effort;
never despise hard work, for it has its benefits
as the book of Proverbs 14:23 confirms:
"All hard work brings a profit,
but mere talk leads only to poverty."
What you sow is what you reap;
always remember that ROUTINE has two destinations:
Where is your ROUTINE leading you to,

FAILURE OR SUCCESS?

BY REVEREND DAVID A.O. IBIAYO

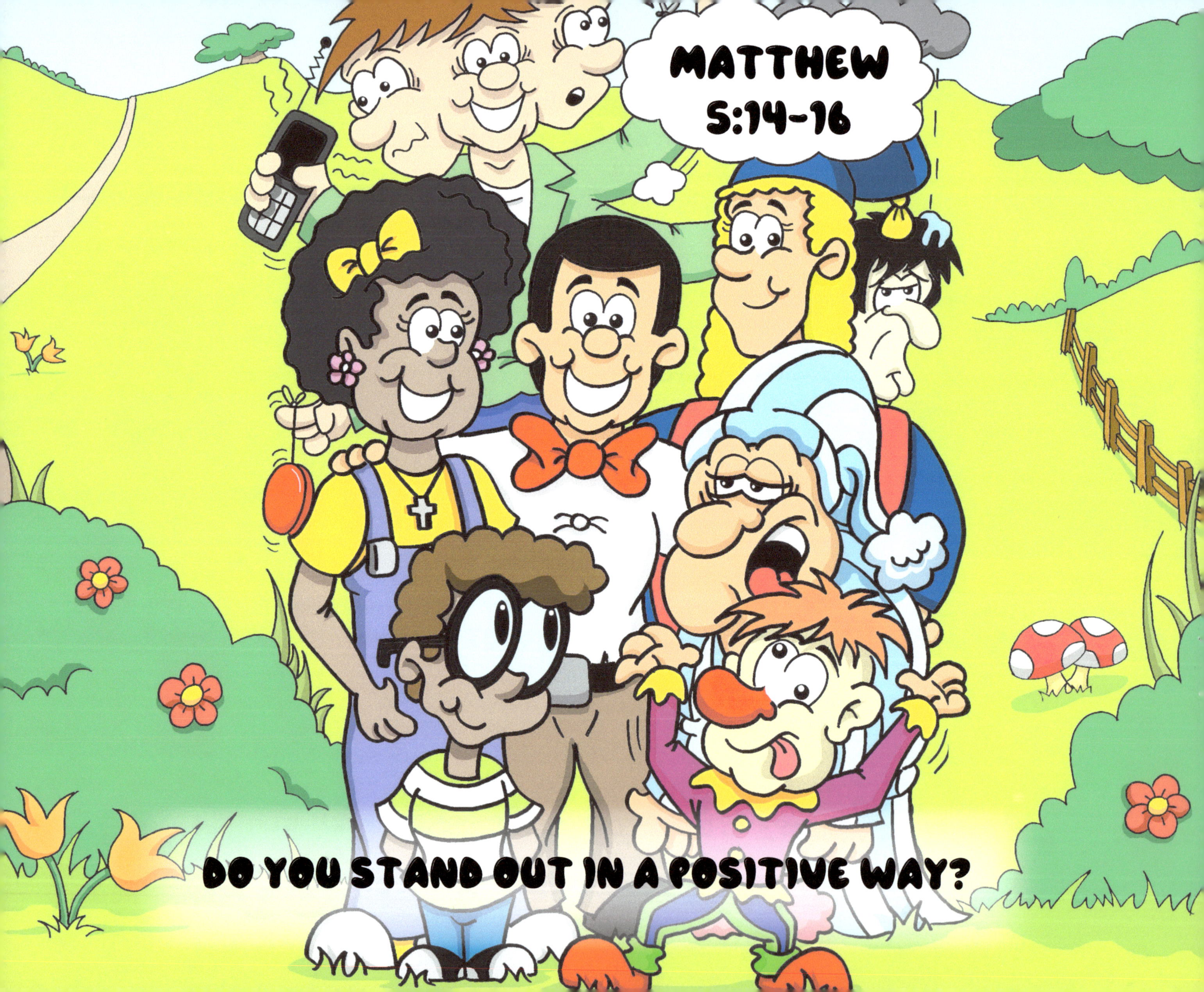
MATTHEW
5:14-16
DO YOU STAND OUT IN A POSITIVE WAY?

www.ingramcontent.com/pod-product-compliance
Lightning Source LLC
Chambersburg PA
CBHW050754090426

42737CB00004B/103

9 781836 150305